TRADING BANKNIFTY OPTIONS

ART OF DOING NOTHING
& STILL MAKING MONEY

TRADING BANKNIFTY OPTIONS

ART OF DOING NOTHING & STILL MAKING MONEY

PRAMOD KUMAR

PRABHAT PRAKASHAN

Published by
PRABHAT PRAKASHAN PVT. LTD.
4/19 Asaf Ali Road,
New Delhi-110 002 (INDIA)
e-mail: prabhatbooks@gmail.com

ISBN 978-93-5562-809-1

TRADING BANKNIFTY OPTIONS: ART OF DOING NOTHING & STILL MAKING MONEY
by Pramod Kumar

Edition
2025

Price
₹ 300 (Rupees Three Hundred only)

Printed at
SS Japan Arts, Delhi

Author's Note

NIFTY and BANKNIFTY options make up the bulk of trading on NSE (National Stock Exchange of India).

Some traders swear by Option Writing or Selling.

They take advantage of the time decay of options for grabbing small profits on consistent basis.

Market participants become so obsessed with the time decay part that they ignore the opportunities presented by Option Buying.

How much chance does an option buyer have to make money?

"As much as a candle in a thunderstorm."

This is the response we get.

Only, it is not a fact.

In this book, we shall have a look at how one can be profitable over long term through buying options in BANKNIFTY.

We shall discuss ATM Call options, ITM Call options, PUT options making money when Black Swan events happen.

This book tells in a very simple manner how a trader can make money without going for complicated strategies.

Simplicity in trading works and makes profit.

Learn the Art of Doing Nothing.

❑

Contents

❑

CHAPTER 1

Secret of Success Lies Within Us

In July 2020, I got a message from a reader of my blog about a strategy to trade in BANKNIFTY.

Well, some call it a strategy. It was buying both the CALL and PUT options of near strike prices and then waiting with it.

This is known as a STRADDLE.

It was mentioned that this method or strategy made money in year 2019 and 2020. Year 2020 was six months gone by that time and the big profit came from the PUT trade in March 2020 series when the big fall happened.

Few days ago, someone shared a long video emphasizing the theme that buying CALL and PUT options both in BANKNIFTY every month could have been profitable over long term.

Why am mentioning both these instances?

It establishes the fact that traders are always looking for a method to make a profit through trading in the market.

There are huge number of videos and books to tell us and teach us how to make a profit through options trading.

Is this book just another one among that huge number?

Yes.

Then why do we need it?

Because, this book does not preach. It narrates the facts in a straightforward manner. Facts which are there all the time for all of us to see, only we ignore them in our quest for a perfect strategy.

A perfect strategy probably does not exist or I am not aware of its existence.

We settle for any method with its blemishes as long as it delivers profits.

And delivers those profits without asking for any mathematical skills on our part.

We are trading for making money, not for getting a degree from a university.

I believe most of the traders are happy to make money without complications. Only when they fail to do so, they look for complex strategies.

Remember the musk deer who just goes round and round searching for the sweet fragrance.

Poor fellow does not know that the fragrance is inside him and any amount of search outside is futile.

Same with traders.

Simple methods of trading success are within us, within the concepts of option definitions. Searching for the holy grail or the perfect strategy will just waste the time and effort.

Simple methods work and work very successfully as I will demonstrate through next few chapters of this book.

What we need along with the method is the belief in what we do and patience to survive the tough times.

We studied the formula for PROFIT in primary classes.

PROFIT = SELL Price – COST Price.

This formula has been in existence since ages. No other formula for profit has yet been invented nor will be done anytime in future.

We need to SELL at a price higher than the BUY price.

We make money, if we do it.

We lose money, if we fail to do it.

Option Buying has the inherent advantage of potential BIG profits and fixed loss.

We are sure about the magnitude of the likely loss but are always on the lookout for maximum profit.

Will buying options work with BANKNIFTY index?

Will we get a decent profit for our efforts?

It could be done with NIFTY options.

That was the theme of my first two books – **PROFIT FROM NIFTY OPTIONS: Art Of Doing Nothing** and **MORE PROFIT FROM NIFTY OPTIONS – Art Of Doing Nothing.**

What is different with BANKNIFTY?

Not much.

Only it is more volatile as compared to NIFTY.

NIFTY is a broad-based index, its constituents taken from various sectors of industries and business.

BANKNIFTY is confined to just banking sector stocks.

That makes it's up and down moves more volatile.

That volatility could be the key for unlocking the trading profits from BANKNIFTY options.

This is enough talk.

Let us walk the talk now.

❑

CHAPTER 2

Banking Stocks Performance over Ten Years

Good stocks give good profit over a long period.

It should be in reverse order.

Stocks that give good profit are called Good stocks.

Let us see how some of the top banking sector stocks have performed over last 10 years.

That gives us a benchmark for comparing our simple method.

Performance Comparison

Scrip	Price 25/10/2012	Price 27/10/2022	Adjusted Price for Splits/ Bonus	%Age Gain/ Loss
HDFCBANK	637.35	1454.50	2908.80	356%
ICICIBANK	1087.15	924.40	5134.20	372%
KOTAKBANK	625.70	1865.00	3730.00	496%
SBIN	2199.85	579.65	5796.50	163%
AXISBANK	1238.05	915.15	4575.75	269%
PNB	803.85	43.00	215.00	(73.25) %
BANKBARODA	769.25	149.70	748.50	(02.00) %
CANBK	441.50	289.60	1448.00	227%
UNIONBANK	208.30	52.90	52.90	(74.60) %
YESBANK	416.20	15.75	78.75	(81.07) %
BANKNIFTY	11614.50	41299.30	41299.30	255.58%

The gains by KOTAKBANK, ICICIBANK and HDFCBANK look impressive and have actually sustained the BANKNIFTY index which has not performed well because of the failure of some stocks.

YESBANK was a constituent of BANKNIFTY not too long ago. It was among the NIFTY 50 stocks as well till its fall from grace.

Index is kept healthy by taking out the stocks that become weak and adding those stocks which are showing strength. That is one reason that the index keeps gaining most of the time.

Investors are not so judicious. They fail to get out of the failed stocks and suffer the consequences.

This is one reason the experts advise to invest in Index Funds.

Usually, investing in the index works out over a period of time.

In this book we shall see how BUYING options in BANKNIFTY month after month performs over a ten years period.

Is it profitable?

Is the performance comparable with the gains made by the index and the top banking sector stocks?

Most people do not believe that option Buying can be profitable. Doing better than index would be something farfetched.

Let us move on to the real numbers.

❑

CHAPTER 3

The First Step Ten Years Ago

On October 25, 2012, BANKNIFTY had closed at 11614.50.

This number looks insignificant compared to the present level of BANKNIFTY but we know that ten years have passed since that date.

If one had bought BANKNIFTY CALL 11600 just before the close of market on that day for November series expiry, the premium paid would have been ₹310.

With a lot size of 25, that would mean an outlay of ₹7750.

We know that options can and do expire worthless. Entire amount of ₹7750 could turn to zero.

We need cushion for bad times (we will have plenty of bad months), hence the capital requirement would be taken as 15 times the first month's takeout.

That would be ₹116250.

We add some more to it and consider ₹125000 as our initial capital.

This is the number we shall use for making comparisons of the results obtained.

BANKNIFTY moved from 11614.50 on October 25, 2012 to 11473.15 on October 31, 2013.

Over the one year period, the index was slightly down.

How did CALL buying perform over the same period?

Market or the index does not move in a predictable straight line method. Moves are random. Occasional big down moves can be followed by sustained up moves. For months together the index may not go anywhere before it just shoots up or sinks down.

Option buyer has the advantage in these situations.

A big move in the desired direction can result in a big profit.

A big move against the desired direction does not cause a loss bigger than the premium amount paid for buying the option.

It is so simple.

It should be profitable too.

Well, there are not many takers for the profitable part of option buying.

In the 12 months period we are discussing here, the highest closing was at 12805.90 on May 30, 2012 and the close on August 29, 2022 was at 8904.60.

This was the year the UPA government was embroiled in 2-G scam and coal block auction scam. It was apparent that the government was on its last legs and there would be a change in the elections to be held in May 2014.

These fears, apprehensions and hopes were reflected in the BANKNIFTY moves.

This is how CALL option buying would have worked.

November 2012- October 2013

Series	BANK-NIFTY at start	BANK-NIFTY at close	ATM CALL strike price	Buy Price	Sell Price	Profit/ Loss
November	11614	11992	11600	310	379	69
December	11992	12459	12000	275	450	175
January	12459	12708	12500	308	213	(95)
February	12708	11487	12700	251	0	(251)
March	11487	11361	11500	290	0	(290)
April	11361	12726	11400	250	1322	1072
May	12726	12805	12700	295	85	(210)
June	12805	11235	12800	261	0	(261)
July	11235	10614	11200	335	0	(335)
August	10614	8904	10600	408	0	(408)
September	8904	10098	8900	410	1193	783
October	10098	11473	10100	475	1367	892
Total						1141

Take note of the contrast in these two situations:

1. In April 2013 series, BANKNIFTY moved from 11361 to 12726. This up move of 1365 points resulted in a profit of 1072 points.
2. In August 2013 series, BANKNIFTY moved lower from 10614 to 8904. The 1710 points fall resulted in a loss of only 408 points.

This loss was made up by the up moves over next two months even though BANKNIFTY did not reach the level before the fall.

Overall, the results of this 12 months period were good with a profit of 1141 points.

This profit came while BANKNIFTY was actually down 141 points for the year

The three big profits ensured that the year was profitable.

Results with ITM (In the Money) Call Options:

Theoretically, ITM Call options should make more profit.

We shall check this assumption with Call options which are about 5% in the money.

Results:

Series	BANK-NIFTY at start	BANK-NIFTY at close	ITM CALL Strike Price	Buy Price	Sell Price	Profit/ Loss
November	11614	11992	11000	738	975	237
December	11992	12459	11400	728	1051	423
January	12459	12708	11900	700	808	108
February	12708	11487	12100	635	0	(635)
March	11487	11361	11000	702	0	(702)
April	11361	12726	10800	700	1917	1217
May	12726	12805	12100	691	707	16
June	12805	11235	12200	690	0	(690)
July	11235	10614	10700	880	0	(880)
August	10614	8904	10000	826	0	(826)
September	8904	10098	8500	650	1591	941
October	10098	11473	9500	865	1967	1102
Total						311

The results are not something to feel very happy about.

Only we should not get disappointed by just one set of numbers.

Let us discuss the logic of going for ITM Call options.

Advantages

In case of a big up move, more points will be captured than what would have been possible with ATM Call options.

In case of small down move, the loss would be limited as the time value of these options would not be too high at the time of buying.

Disadvantage

If there is a big down move, the loss will be really big as the ITM Call options come at a very hefty premium.

This is what happened here.

There were five occasions when the options became worthless.

In case of ATM options, the loss was less whereas ITM options lost out big amounts.

Putting more money in buying the options did not result in better profits.

What do we conclude from these numbers?

One year of profit does not prove any theory.

We need much more data to back our claim that CALL option buying in BANKNIFTY could be profitable.

Next year would be 2014 which we know was the election year when BJP government came to power and the markets moved up.

If CALL option buying was profitable while BANKNIFTY was slightly down over 12 months, next 12 months should be very good.

We do the analysis in the next chapter.

❑

CHAPTER 4

New Government Comes In – Market Moves Higher

I am a votary of the theory that the governments actually do not matter for the market moves over a long period of time.

But long periods of time comprises of many short periods of time.

Elections, government policies, budget presentations and many other factors come into play in these short time periods. This adds volatility to the option prices and buying of options becomes costly at such times.

What can we do about it?

Nothing much. We just accept the harsh reality of option pricing and live with the fact.

2014 was the election year in India and the journey through these 12 months was exciting.

November 2013

BANKNIFTY moved lower in this series.

Series began at 11473 and closed at 10906. ATM Call 11500 priced at ₹355 at the beginning of the series became worthless.

Loss – 355 Points.

December 2013

ATM Call strike for December 2013 series was 10900.

BANKNIFTY moved to 11385 at the end of series but the move did not result into any big gain.

Buy Price – 441 Sell Price – 480

Profit – 39 Points.

With this we move into the new year 2014.

January 2014

The usual option buyer's luck or bad luck continued in January series as BANKNIFTY went down from 11385 to 10153.

This fall of 1232 points (10.82%) in one month caused a loss of 394 points as CALL 11400 went on to become worthless from the buying price of ₹394.

An investor in BANKNIFTY would have lost 1232 points.

Loss of ATM Call buyer was ₹394.

Loss – 394 Points.

February 2014

In February series, BANKNIFTY recovered a part of the fall seen in the previous month as it moved from 10153 to 10730.

ATM Call 10200 moved up from ₹315 to ₹539.

Profit – 224 Points.

March 2014

This month saw a big surge in the market. By this time, it was a foregone conclusion that UPA government was on the way out in the elections to be conducted soon.

Market runs on sentiment and the sentiment was bullish.

BANKNIFTY began the series at 10730 and closed at 12804.

A gain of 2074 points (19.32%).

BANKNIFTY CALL 10700 priced at ₹289 finally ended up at ₹1905.

A huge profit for the option buyer.

We saw in January 2014 series that a 1232-point fall had caused a loss of 394 points.

In March 2014, the 2074-points gain in BANKNIFTY resulted in a profit of 1616 points.

These are the perfect examples of LIMITED LOSS, UNLIMITED PROFIT for an option buyer.

Such months will be few and will be spaced far apart but that is the time to cash the big profit.

Profit – 1616 Points.

April 2014

Nation was in election mode. Governance came to a standstill. Market had already moved significantly higher in the previous series. In April, BANKNIFTY moved from 12804 to 13122.

A small move compared to the big jump in the last month.

BANKNIFTY Call 12800 priced at ₹337 closed at ₹318 on expiry.

Option buyer can lose money even when the directional move is right but not big enough to cover the premium paid.

Loss – 19 Points.

May 2014

Election time.

Results were to be announced in the middle of the month.

Option premiums were sky high.

One has to pay the price for optimism.

BANKNIFTY CALL 13100 was priced at `680 at the beginning of the series. This premium was more than double of what was paid in April series.

As expected, NDA led by BJP came to power.

By the end of May series, BANKNIFTY had moved up to 15030.

Call 13100 was at ₹1917 at the end.

Even while paying a hefty premium for buying the CALL, profit for May series come to ₹1237.

A good month.

Profit – 1237 Points.

June 2014

New government was in place.

Market euphoria died down.

BANKNIFTY was flat for June series at it began at 15030 and closed at 15050.

A flat month is as bad as a month with a big fall for the CALL buyer as the quantum of loss remains the same.

BANKNIFTY Call 15000 worth ₹474 closed at ₹46.

Loss – 428 Points

July 2014

Once again it was a dull series as BANKNIFTY gained just 217 points.

Series began at 15050 and closed at 15267.

Premium paid for CALL 15000 was not a total loss as ₹268 could be salvaged out of initial premium of ₹595.

Loss – 327 Points.

August 2014

The flat trend continued for August series too.

Index moved up from 15267 to 15740.

This can be considered a normal move but having seen the big jumps in March and May, this looks insignificant.

BANKNIFTY CALL 15300 moved up from ₹360 to ₹425.

Not a very big gain but still a profit.

Profit – 65 Points.

September 2014

After three months of small gains, BANKNIFTY decided to give up some ground in September series.

It fell from 15740 to 15299.

This move took away the entire premium of ₹330 paid for BANKNIFT CALL 15700.

Option buyers are always warned about options expiring worthless. This was another such occasion.

Loss – 330 Points.

October 2014

Finally, a good month arrived.

This time, BANKNIFTY moved decidedly higher as it crossed 16000 level and closed the series at 16760.

ATM BANKNIFTY Call 15300 saw its price move up from ₹425 to ₹1465 resulting in a good profit.

Profit – 1040 Points.

Summary of 12 Months is tabulated here:

November 2013 – October 2014

Series	BANK-NIFTY at start	BANK-NIFTY at close	ATM CALL strike price	Buy Price	Sell Price	Profit/ Loss
November	11473	10906	11500	355	0	(355)
December	10906	11385	10900	441	480	39
January	11385	10153	11400	394	0	(394)
February	10153	10730	10200	315	539	224
March	10730	12804	10700	289	1905	1616
April	12804	13122	12800	337	318	(19)
May	13122	15030	13100	680	1917	1237

June	15030	15050	15000	474	46	(428)
July	15050	15267	15000	595	268	(327)
August	15267	15740	15300	360	425	65
September	15740	15299	15700	330	0	(330)
October	15299	16760	15300	425	1465	1040
Total						2368

These 12 months had 6 losers and 6 gainers. Number of worthless trades was 3.

It was the big gains in March, May and October series which made this period profitable.

ITM Call Options

We saw that the profit through ITM Call options in the previous year was not very good.

With BANKNIFTY moving from 11473 to 16760, the result should be good this time.

Here are the numbers:

Series	BANK-NIFTY at start	BANK-NIFTY at close	ITM CALL strike price	Buy Price	Sell Price	Profit/Loss
November	11473	10906	10900	723	0	(723)
December	10906	11385	10400	716	980	264

January	11385	10153	10800	790	0	(790)
February	10153	10730	9600	519	726	207
March	10730	12804	10200	635	2395	1760
April	12804	13122	12200	690	910	220
May	13122	15030	12500	1031	2528	1497
June	15030	15050	14200	1050	850	(200)
July	15050	15267	14200	1100	1200	100
August	15267	15740	14500	900	1240	340
Septem-ber	15740	15299	15000	825	277	(548)
October	15299	16760	14500	944	2250	1606
Total						3733

This time returns from ITM Call options are better than those from ATM Call options.

This is how it should work out most of the time but there will be exceptions from time to time.

The first two years have shown very decent profitability through Call buying.

Will it always work?

The story continues in next chapter.

❑

CHAPTER 5

The Testing Times

Option buying makes money only when we get a good directional move. Small moves do not work out as these are generally not enough to cover the premium amount paid for buying the option.

If the Index moves within a narrow range for some time, that time is not good for option buyers.

We learn that lesson in this chapter as the journey through next 12 months from November 2014 to October 2015 is described.

November 2014

We pick up from where we left in October series.

BANKNIFTY Call 16800 for November Series was priced at ₹338 at the close of October series trades.

The index moved up from 16760 to 18022 in November.

Sell Price – ₹1208

Profit – 870 Points.

December 2014

December series had BANKNIFTY moving from 18022 to 18535.

We have seen earlier that these 2-3% type of gains do not yield much by way of profit.

This time too was not different.

CALL 18000 went up from ₹473 to ₹515.

Profit – 42 Points

January 2015

The first month of the new year 2015 turned out to be very good for the index as it moved from 18535 to 20528 thus gaining 1997 points.

These 10% kind of moves do not happen every time but are welcome when they do.

CALL 18500 made a similar good move from ₹595 to ₹2015.

Profit – 1420 Points.

February 2015

There is a saying – “Whatever goes up must come down.”

This came true immediately as BANKNIFTY fell from 20528 to 18538 in this series.

Gain of 1997 points was surrendered with 1990 points down move this time.

Call 20500 lost the entire premium of ₹631 as it became worthless.

Loss – 631 Points.

March 2015

I remember March 2015 very distinctly as I had made very good profit in that month by buying PUT options.

Here we are talking about buying CALL options.

Naturally, the month that was good for PUT trades will not give anything to CALL buyers.

One significant point in this series was that on March 04, 2015 NIFTY made the then ALL TIME HIGH of 9119.20 and SENSEX crossed 30000 level for the first time.

Also significant is the point that on the day of these record highs, market actually closed in the red.

And the down trend continued till February of 2016.

We had BANKNIFTY at 18538 as the March series commenced. CALL 18500 was priced at `668.

At the end of series, BANKNIFTY was at 17831 and CALL 18500 was worthless.

Loss - 668 Points.

April 2015

April series saw some recovery after the disappointment of February and March series.

BANKNIFTY moved higher from 17831 to 18338.

It is nowhere near to 20528 seen at the end of January series.

CALL 17800 failed to make a profit as its initial price of ₹612 went down to ₹532 when the series ended.

Loss – 80 Points.

May 2015

By this time, NDA government was almost one year old. Market had by now got into the routine and it was business as normal.

May series was absolutely flat as BANKNIFTY moved from 18338 to 18449.

Nothing could be gained from such a small movement.

CALL 18300 went down from ₹556 to ₹147.

Loss – 409 Points

June 2015

Trading becomes tough when we face consecutive losses. Option buyers have to bear this fact in mind that they will have more losing trades than the winners. And many of the losses will be coming just one after the other. It is easy to state this fact but bearing the pain of regular losses can be difficult.

June was another flat series with BANKNIFTY going from 18449 to 18492.

Another wasted month as CALL 18400 was worth only ₹97 at the end from its buy price of ₹551.

Loss – 454 Points.

July 2015

July was no improvement over previous month.

This time the move was on the downside. A small move, from 18492 to 18440.

For three months BANKNIFTY was stagnating.

May series had begun with the index at 18338 and July close was 18440.

Such moves have only one possible outcome – a loss.

There was another loss of 482 points as CALL 18500 became worthless.

Loss – 482 Points.

August 2015

Well, this month was not flat.

There was a big fall as BANKNIFTY went down from 18440 to 17214. The fall was 1226 points.

The extent of fall does not matter.

We lost the entire premium amount when there was a small decline of 52 points in July and we again lose the entire premium when the fall is 1226 points.

Call 18400 went from ₹485 to 0.

Loss – 485 Points.

September 2015

With a number of losses booked, we look for any significant up move.

To take advantage of any likely move, one has to be in the trade.

At the beginning of the series, CALL 17200 was priced at ₹577.

Once again,we saw the option becoming worthless with a very small change in the index.

The move was from 17214 to 17196.

A trifling move but enough to cause a loss.

Loss – 577 Points.

October 2015

Most of the option traders are not big fans of option buying. And with the kind of results seen in 2015, nobody would blame them.

October series was September in reverse.

This time BANKNIFTY moved from 17196 to 17212.

The movement was reverse of the previous month but the result was same.

CALL 17200 went down from ₹600 to ₹3.00.

Loss – 597 Points.

With this our tale of woes for this year comes to a close.

Summary of 12 Months:

November 2014- October 2015

Series	BANK-NIFTY at start	BANK-NIFTY at close	ATM Call strike price	Buy Price	Sell Price	Profit/ Loss
November	16760	18022	16800	338	1208	870
December	18022	18535	18000	473	515	42
January	18535	20528	18500	595	2015	1420
February	20528	18538	20500	631	0	(631)
March	18538	17831	18500	668	0	(668)
April	17831	18338	17800	612	532	(80)
May	18338	18449	18300	556	147	(409)
June	18449	18492	18400	551	97	(454)

July	18492	18440	18500	482	0	(482)
August	18440	17214	18400	485	0	(485)
September	17214	17196	17200	577	0	(577)
October	17196	17212	17200	600	3	(597)
Total						(2051)

There were 3 profits and 9 losses in these 12 months, the losses all coming consecutively.

All the profit of first three months was gone soon and ultimately resulted in a big loss of 2051 points.

For this 12-month period, BANKNIFTY was up only 452 points. This fact did not help in making any profit from CALL buying.

The five occasions when the options became worthless added a very good number to the total loss.

In the previous two years, we checked the performance of ITM Call option buying.

As BANKNIFTY kept moving in a narrow range for few months, ITM Call options became worthless only on two occasions.

The loss was comparably lower in May, June and July series.

The final outcome was still a loss.

ITM Call Options

Series	BANK-NIFTY at start	BANK-NIFTY at close	ITM Call strike price	Buy Price	Sell Price	Profit/ Loss
November	16760	18022	16000	900	2012	1112
December	18022	18535	17000	1195	1556	361
January	18535	20528	17500	1320	3068	1748
February	20528	18538	19500	1311	0	(1311)
March	18538	17831	17500	1330	312	(1018)
April	17831	18338	17000	1217	1335	118
May	18338	18449	17500	1126	949	(177)
June	18449	18492	17500	1155	996	(159)
July	18492	18440	17500	1150	934	(216)
August	18440	17214	17500	1100	0	(1100)
September	17214	17196	16500	1044	689	(355)
October	17196	17212	16500	1051	699	(352)
Total						(1359)

This year was a reality check.

Option buying is not a one way ticket to profit.

There is pain of losses to be suffered at times.

We have to keep the belief and keep trading.

Over to next 12 months.

❑

CHAPTER 6

The Tough Choice

Trading is a wonderful activity while we are making a profit. It is a challenge when things go wrong.

We had many trades going wrong over past few months.

The same trend of BANKNIFTY not going anywhere continued in November and December series of year 2016.

November 2016

We saw a small down move in this series from 17212 to 17036.

Call 17200 moved from ₹480 to 0.

Loss – 480 Points.

December 2016

Similar story again.

BANKNIFTY moved from 17036 to 16922.

Call 17000 went from ₹515 to 0.

Loss – 515 Points.

We welcome the new year 2016 after very bad experience of Call option buying in 2015.

January 2016

The appalling luck with Call buying continued in the first month of the new year.

This time BANKNIFTY had a big fall from 16922 to 15381.

Call 16900 caused a loss of 345 points as it became worthless.

Loss -- 345 Points

February 2016

Another big fall was waiting for us in February 2016 series.

BANKNIFTY crashed to 13555 as the series came to a close.

Call 15400 priced at ₹440 ended up worthless.

March 2016

With 13 consecutive losses, even the most hopeful of traders would be on the edge of desperation.

Is the method flawed?

Let us look at the bright side of the dark picture.

BANKNIFTY had fallen from 20528 (January 2015 series closing) to 13555 (February 2016 series closing).

Anyone investing in BANKNIFTY ETF would have lost 6973 points.

ATM Call buying suffered losses but those losses are smaller when compared to these 6973 points.

In March series, BANKNIFTY recovered from the dismal level of 13555 to 16141.

The gain was 2586 points or 19.07%.

Finally, a light at the end of dark tunnel of losses.

CALL 13600 moved up to ₹2525 from its initial price of ₹452.

Profit – 2073 Points.

This single profit wiped out the loss incurred over previous four months.

April 2016

BANKNIFTY continued the up move in April series but the gain was not much.

It moved from 16141 to 16716.

CALL 16100 moved from ₹514 to ₹613.

Profit – 99 Points.

May 2016

Another up move from 16716 to 17359 saw BANKNIFTY CALL 16700 gain a profit of ₹211 as its price went up to ₹646 from ₹435.

Profit – 211 Points.

June 2016

BANKNIFTY was covering the lost ground over last few months. It had a lot to cover.

In June series, the index went up from 17359 to 17935.

Small gains do not bring windfall profits but keep us in the game.

Any profit is better than taking a loss.

CALL 17400 moved from ₹359 to ₹515.

Profit – 156 Points.

July 2016

Last 4 months gave some profits.

We have a long way to go to cover the losses seen in the 13 months prior to that.

Only way to do that is keep trading.

In July, BANKNIFTY made a better move as it went up to 19076 from 17935 of previous close.

CALL 17900 went up from ₹422 to ₹1162.

Profit – 740 Points.

August 2016

BANKNIFTY had covered the distance from 13555 to 19076 in the last 5 months.

August was a breather as the index inched its way to 19304 to close the series.

CALL 19000 priced at ₹474 ended up at ₹393 causing a loss.

Loss – 181 Points.

September 2016

We were once again faced with a flat series for BANKNIFTY.

The move was from 19304 to 19183.

Such moves have only one outcome – a loss.

CALL 19300 priced at ₹404 became worthless.

Loss – 404 Points.

October 2016:

Small moves continued. This time the move was on the higher side.

BANKNIFTY closed the October series at 19514.

CALL 19200 initially priced at ₹520 returned only ₹300 at the end causing another loss.

Loss – 220 Points.

Summary of 12 Months:

November 2015 – October 2016:

Series	BANK-NIFTY at start	BANK-NIFTY at close	ATM Call strike price	Buy Price	Sell Price	Profit/ Loss
November	17212	17036	17200	480	0	(480)
December	17036	16922	17000	515	0	(515)
January	16922	15381	16900	345	0	(345)
February	15381	13555	15400	440	0	(440)
March	13555	16141	13600	452	2525	2073
April	16141	16716	16100	514	613	99
May	16716	17359	16700	435	646	211
June	17359	17935	17400	359	515	156
July	17935	19076	17900	422	1162	740
August	19076	19304	19000	474	293	(181)
September	19304	19183	19300	404	0	(404)
October	19183	19514	19200	520	300	(220)
Total						694

Eventually, there was a profit of 694 points over these 12 months but not before facing serious trouble with 13 consecutive losses.

If the trading was done with ITM Call options, the result would have been slightly better. We have tabulated the results for three previous years. Here are the results for the 12 months from November 2015 to October 2016.

ITM Call Options:

Series	BANK-NIFTY at start	BANK-NIFTY at close	ITM Call strike price	Buy Price	Sell Price	Profit/ Loss
November	17212	17036	16500	937	535	(402)
December	17036	16922	16200	986	721	(265)
January	16922	15381	16200	870	0	(870)
February	15381	13555	14500	1019	0	(1019)
March	13555	16141	13000	815	3135	2320
April	16141	16716	15200	1181	1511	330
May	16716	17359	16000	905	1387	462
June	17359	17935	16500	930	1417	487
July	17935	19076	17000	1072	2063	991
August	19076	19304	18000	1199	1292	93
September	19304	19183	18200	1395	1172	(223)
October	19183	19514	18200	1397	1510	113
Total						2017

Profit From ITM Call options was better at 2017 points though the losses from November to February would have hurt badly.

I mentioned about keeping the belief earlier.

It is not easy to keep the belief when facing consecutive losses.

Losses disturb a trader and disrupt the thought process. At such times, we go back to thoughts like – "Option buyers never make money."

And most of the traders quit at this point.

By now they are convinced that option buying is for dummies and no good can ever come out of it.

Life of a trader is about making the tough choice.

The tough choice like quitting or continuing.

We know that quitters never win and winners do not quit.

This saying is not without reason.

There is a very popular story of King Bruce and the spider.

Option buyers need the same tenacity.

Let us find out what happens to those who do not quit. Do they really turn out winners in the long term?

❑

CHAPTER 7

Good Times Once Again

We have completed four years of this study whether BANKNIFTY Call buying month after month and doing nothing after that can lead to any profits.

A quick summary seems to be in order at this time.

Year November - October	ATM Call Option Points	ATM Call Profit Months	ITM Call Option Points	ITM Call Profit Months
2012-13	1141	5	311	7
2013-14	2368	6	3733	8
2014-15	(2051)	3	(1359)	4

2015-16	694	5	2017	7
Total	2152	19	4702	26

In these four years BANKNIFTY moved up from 11614 to 19514, a gain of 7900 points.

ATM Call buying could get 2152 points with 19 successful trades out of 48.

ITM Call buying gave better results by capturing 4702 points with 26 successful trades out of 48.

One bad year not withstanding, the results are fairly good.

We now move on to fifth year of doing the same thing.

November 2016

A steep fall from 19514 to 18256 was what we got in November 2016 series.

It took away the entire premium of CALL 19500 priced at ₹434.

Loss – 434 Points.

December 2016

If the fall in November was steep, December series was almost flat as BANKNIFTY declined from 18256 to 18033.

For the buyer of Call option, pain is same whether the fall is big or small.

BANKNIFTY Call 18300 moved from ₹441 to 0.

Another losing month.

Loss – 441 Points

January 2017

New year 2017 brought some cheer to Call buyers as BANKNIFTY made a smart recovery from 18033 to 19473.

This move was good enough for CALL 18000 price to move up from ₹381 to 1477.

Profit – 1096 Points.

February 2017

The uptrend in BANKNIFTY continued in February series too. The level of 20500 seen two years ago was taken out as the index moved from 19473 to 20876.

CALL 19500 moved up from ₹390 to ₹1378.

Profit – 988 Points

March 2017

BANKNIFTY had momentum now.

In this series, 21500 level too was taken out. The expiry for March series was at 21620.

CALL 20900 reached a price of ₹716 from its initial buy price of ₹376.

Profit – 340 Points

April 2017

In April series, BANKNIFTY continued moving higher and closed at 22326.

The move was not very big but good enough to chalk out a decent profit.

Call 21600 Buy Price – ₹246 Sell Price – ₹728

Profit – 472 Points

May 2017

New year had begun with BANKNIFTY closing at 18033 in December 2016 series.

In four months since then, it was at 22326.

More than 4000 points gained. Life was good for Call option buying.

The uptrend continued in May series as BANKNIFTY moved up to 23190.

CALL 22300 which had an initial price of ₹315 finally ended up at ₹855.

Profit – 540 Points

June 2017

All good things come to an end.

June was the month which halted the uptrend.

It was not exactly stopped but the gain was a measly 37 points.

From 23190 to 23227 is not much of a move for an index known for its volatile moves.

CALL 23200 went down in price from ₹255 to ₹23.

Loss – 232 Points.

July 2017

After a flat month in June, BANKNIFTY gathered momentum once again and moved from 23227 to 24992 at the end of July series.

A good month to be in Call buying.

CALL 23200 shot up to ₹1721 from the initial price of ₹355.

Profit – 1366 Points

August 2017

BANKNIFTY was at 24992.

Hopes were soaring for the new high.

But August series was a damp squib as the index came down to 24318.

CALL 25000 became worthless.

That was ₹360 gone waste like most bought options do.

Loss – 360 Points

September 2017

BANKNIFTY moved further down in September.

The move was not big.

Only 24318 to 24008.

CALL 24300 lost the entire premium amount of ₹391.

Loss – 391 Points.

October 2017

On October 24, 2017, the Finance Minister made a big announcement about recapitalization of public sector banks.

Next day saw stocks like BANKBARODA, PNB, SBIN move up 40-50%.

Even with their low weight in BANKNIFTY, the big moves caused the index to move higher.

It closed the series at 25022 after beginning at 24008.

CALL 24000 – Buy Price – ₹393 Sell Price – ₹1012

Profit – 619 Points.

Summary of 12 Months

November 2016 – October 2017

Series	BANK-NIFTY at start	BANK-NIFTY at close	ATM Call strike price	Buy Price	Sell Price	Profit/ Loss
November	19514	18256	19500	434	0	(434)
December	18256	18033	18300	441	0	(441)
January	18033	19473	18000	381	1477	1096

February	19473	20876	19500	390	1378	988
March	20876	21620	20900	376	716	340
April	21620	22326	21600	246	728	472
May	22326	23190	22300	315	855	540
June	23190	23227	23200	255	23	(232)
July	23227	24922	23200	355	1721	1366
August	24922	24318	25000	360	0	(360)
September	24318	24008	24300	391	0	(391)
October	24008	25022	24000	393	1012	619
Total						3563

A profit of 3563 points over 12 months is a very good outcome. There were 5 losses and 7 profits.

BANKNIFTY went up by 5508 points and ATM Call buying could cash 3563 points from this move.

Results from ITM Call buying were even better.

They are tabulated here:

ITM Call Options

Series	BANK-NIFTY at start	BANK-NIFTY at close	ITM Call strike price	Buy Price	Sell Price	Profit/ Loss
November	19514	18256	18500	1173	0	(1173)
December	18256	18033	17500	1070	514	(556)
January	18033	19473	17000	1140	2470	1340
February	19473	20876	18500	1090	2365	1175
March	20876	21620	20000	960	1630	670
April	21620	22326	20500	1060	1815	755
May	22326	23190	21000	1298	2186	888
June	23190	23227	22000	1099	1222	223
July	23227	24922	22000	1270	2900	1630
August	24922	24318	24000	1094	316	(738)
September	24318	24008	23000	1384	1010	(374)
October	24008	25022	23000	1114	2007	893
Total						4733

With 8 profits and 4 losses, total profit comes to 4733 points.

Year number 5 was very good.

We move on to sixth year of doing nothing.

❑

CHAPTER 8

Twelve Months of Nothingness

The story so far has been simple, profitable and repetitive.

It may be boring as well.

We can live with the boring part as long as profits keep coming. In fact, profitable trading is generally boring. Seekers of excitement should venture into other activities like para jumping or scuba diving.

The story continues.

November 2017

Peak 25000 was scaled in October 2017 series.

Not much movement happened in November as BANKNIFTY crawled its way from 25022 to 25332.

CALL 25000 came down in value from ₹469 to ₹311.

Loss – 158 Points

December 2017

December series too had gone the same way with BANKNIFTY covering the distance from 25332 to 25490.

CALL 25300 lost out ₹341 as its price fell from ₹500 to ₹159.

Loss – 341 Points.

January 2018

After the dull moves over last two months, BANKNIFTY made a big jump in the first month of new year 2018.

The move was big – from 25490 to 27445.

A good opportunity to book a profit from CALL option buying.

CALL 25500 moved from ₹336 to ₹1927.

Profit – 1591 Points.

February 2018

In February there was a big fall and the entire gains made by the index in January were given back.

BANKNIFTY fell from 27445 to 24955.

BANKNIFTY had gained 1955 points in January and lost 2490 points in February.

The profit from January gain was 1591 points and the loss caused due to the fall in February was 506 points as CALL 27400 became worthless.

This is the edge enjoyed by option buyers.

In case of a big move against their trade, the loss is LIMITED.

Loss – 506 Points.

March 2018

BANKNIFTY declined further to 24263 in March series.

CALL 25000 bought at ₹465 ended up at 0.

Loss – 465 Points.

April 2018

April series brought some relief as the market moved higher and BANKNIFTY moved from 24263 to 25010.

CALL 24300 went up from ₹505 to ₹710.

Profit – 205 Points.

In six months, BANKNIFTY had moved from 25022 to 25010.

With the up and down moves combined ATM Call buying made some money in this flat journey of the index.

May 2018

There was a big jump in May 2018.

From 25010 to 26956.

Option buyers always wish for such moves only to get them on few occasions.

CALL 25000 saw its price move up from ₹458 to ₹1965.

Profit – 1507 Points

June 2018

After the big move in May, it was time for the index to cool down and it went down from 26956 to 26324.

CALL 27000 became worthless and lost the entire premium of ₹319.

Loss – 319 Points

July 2018

The see-saw moves continued in July.

This time BANKNIFTY reached 27400 level once again and closed at 27406.

CALL 26300 went up to ₹1085 from its initial price of ₹365.

Profit – 720 Points.

August 2018

BANKNIFTY moved from 27406 to 28103 in this series.

This move was good enough for getting a profit of 230 points as CALL 27400 moved up in price from ₹462 to ₹692.

Profit – 230 Points

September 2018

September 2018 was the month when banking and financial sector stocks went into a tailspin because of huge default by IL&FS Limited, an infrastructure company which announced that it will not be able to pay its debt liabilities.

DHFL stock was the worst sufferer and others like IBULHSGFIN, L&TFH too faced the music.

Most of the banking stocks went down and the result was a 3061-point crash in this series.

Fortunately, option buyers can not lose more than the premium amount paid.

CALL 28100 priced initially at ₹458 became worthless.

Loss – 458 Points.

October 2018

BANKNIFTY lost few more points in October series as banking stocks were subdued after the punishment received in September.

It went down from 25042 to 24817.

CALL 25000 lost the full premium amount of ₹665.

Loss – 665 Points.

Summary of the year

November 2017- October 2018

Series	BANK-NIFTY at start	BANK-NIFTY at close	ATM Call strike price	Buy Price	Sell Price	Profit/ Loss
November	25022	25332	25000	469	311	(158)
December	25332	25490	25300	500	159	(341)
January	25490	27445	25500	336	1927	1591
February	27445	24955	27400	506	0	(506)
March	24955	24263	25000	465	0	(465)
April	24263	25010	24300	505	710	205
May	25010	26956	25000	458	1965	1507
June	26956	26324	27000	319	0	(319)
July	26324	27406	26300	365	1085	720
August	27406	28103	27400	462	692	230
September	28103	25042	28100	458	0	(458)
October	25042	24817	25000	665	0	(665)
Total						1341

BANKNIFTY had moved from 25022 to 24817 in these 12 months.

There were big down moves and big up moves.

Profit from the up moves was more than the loss suffered due to down moves.

Out of 12 months, 5 were profitable and total profit was 1341 points.

On 5 occasions, options became worthless.

Considering that the index actually went nowhere, this is a very good profit.

ITM Call Option Buying

We check these numbers as well as we did for previous years.

Series	BANK-NIFTY at start	BANK-NIFTY at close	ITM Call strike price	Buy Price	Sell Price	Profit/ Loss
November	25022	25332	24000	1175	1335	160
December	25332	25490	24000	1496	1480	(16)
January	25490	27445	24500	1050	2950	1940
February	27445	24955	26000	1421	0	(1421)
March	24955	24263	24000	1139	253	(876)
April	24263	25010	23000	1448	2006	558
May	25010	26956	24000	1158	2940	1782
June	26956	26324	25500	1340	800	(540)

July	26324	27406	25000	1321	2380	1059
August	27406	28103	26000	1520	2095	575
September	28103	25042	26500	1740	0	(1740)
October	25042	24817	24000	1425	800	(625)
Total						856

For a change, the profit from ATM CALL options turned out to be higher.

The only reason appears to be the higher premium amount going worthless on two occasions.

Such anomalies will occur from time to time.

This was another year of profits for BANKNIFTY CALL buying.

With results for six years in the bag, we should be able to conclude that CALL buying in BANKNIFTY is a profitable way to trade.

We keep that conclusion in abeyance for now and move forward with the story.

❑

CHAPTER 9

Life Gets Tough Before It Becomes Easy

In six years, BANKNIFTY had moved from 11614 to 24817.

It was in line with the theory that over a long period index moves higher.

Let us briefly review the results of six years of CALL buying in BANKNIFTY.

Year November - October	ATM Call Option Points	ATM Call Profit Months	ITM Call Option Points	ITM Call Profit Months
2012-13	1141	5	311	7
2013-14	2368	6	3733	8
2014-15	(2051)	3	(1359)	4
2015-16	694	5	2017	7
2016-17	3563	7	4733	8
2017-18	1341	5	856	6
Total	7056	31	10291	40

ATM Call option buying captured 7056 profit points out of total BANKNIFTY gain of 13203 points.

ITM Call option buying profit at 10291 points is real bonanza.

Yet, people tell us that option buying is not the way to make money in the market.

Those kinds of thoughts are not going to change anytime soon, the bias against option buying being very strong.

It is our job to paint the right picture, it is up to the viewers whether they look at the beauty of it.

In the period, November 2018 to October 2019, BANKNIFTY moved higher, from 24817 to 30066.

These numbers straightway tell us that these 12 months would have been good for CALL option buyers.

Let us find out how the index completed this journey on month-to-month basis.

In this period, we saw Lok Sabha elections, a new finance minister finding her way amidst challenges of the economy and many more problems.

November 2018

November series was very good for BANKNIFTY.

Market overlooked the troubles of September 2018 and marched ahead with determination. BANKNIFTY moved from 24817 to 26939, a gain of 2122 points.

CALL 24800 Buy Price – ₹822 Sell Price – ₹2144

Profit –1322 Points.

December 2018

December series turned out to be flat with BANKNIFTY going down from 26939 to 26878.

We know what happens in such situations.

CALL 26900 priced at ₹453 became worthless.

Loss – 453 Points.

January 2019

This was a positive month for the index with BANKNIFTY moving from 26878 to 27245.

Still, it was not good enough to make a profit.

CALL 26900 went down to ₹380 from its buy price of ₹550.

Loss – 170 Points

February 2019

This series began at 27245 and closed at 26789.

With BANKNIFTY moving lower, there was no way CALL 27200 could make money. That was another premium of ₹475 becoming worthless.

Loss – 475 Points

March 2019

Lok Sabha elections were in the air.

In place of regular Union Budget, a vote on account was presented in the parliament by Mr. Piyush Goyal, who had taken charge of Finance Ministry after the passing away of Mr. Arun Jaitley.

It was a combination of the budget proposals, anticipation of BJP victory in the upcoming elections or just dumb luck which made BANKNIFTY really shoot up in March series.

It went up to 30420.

From 26789 to 30420 meant a gain of 3631 points.

This gain worked out wonderfully for CALL 26800 as its price shot up to ₹3600 from initial ₹631.

Profit – 2969 Points.

April 2019

Elections were round the corner but the buzz of the previous series had died down.

BANKNIFTY lost some ground and moved lower to 29561 to close the series.

CALL 30400 went down to zero from ₹690.

Loss – 690 Points.

May 2019

Election time.

The time when option premiums become sky high.

Even if you get the move in the right direction, profit is not much. If you end up on the wrong side, the loss is quite big.

BJP victory was considered a certainty. Even then, the premium for CALL 29600 was substantial at ₹1025.

After the results, there was an up move and BANKNIFTY closed the May series at 31537.

CALL 29600 had moved to ₹1914.

Profit – 889 Points.

June 2019

A new Finance Minister, Ms. Nirmala Seetharaman had taken over the charge of the finance ministry.

Election was over, it was back to nitty gritty of governance.

Market too resumed into its normal mode.

June series saw BANKNIFTY move lower from 31537 to 31269.

CALL 31500 became worthless and the premium of ₹635 was gone.

Loss – 635 Points.

July 2019

Remember the statement made by the Finance Minister about the millennials not buying cars and travelling by Ola and Uber cabs.

This was her reasoning for the decline in car sales numbers.

Whether the economy was suffering from post election syndrome or poor monsoons or whatever else, this was a real bad month for banking stocks and BANKNIFTY.

From 31269 it plummeted down to 29043.

This number was lower than the closing number of April series.

This meant another loss of ₹563 as CALL 31300 became worthless.

Loss – 563 Points.

August 2019

People had expected big up move in the market after the emphatic BJP victory in the elections.

That expectation did not come true.

In August, another effort at recapitalization of public sector was made. There was a merger of 10 PSU banks into 4 entities. All this was supposed to lend a boost to the market.

Market failed to respond to these measures and BANKNIFTY made a further slide to 27309 level.

We had CALL 29000 going from ₹657 to 0.

Loss - 657 Points.

September 2019

With BANKNIFTY down to 27309 from May close of 31537 and market not showing any sign of recovery, the Finance Minister was really under pressure.

If her press conference in August failed to enthuse the market, September turned out to be a different story.

In the press conference on September 20, 2019 many tax concessions were announced for the industry. As if the market was waiting for some cue, BANKNIFTY shot up.

The move was from 26757 on September 19 to 28981 on September 20.

A gain of 2224 points in a single day.

September series closed at 30002.

BANKNIFTY CALL 27300 made very good gains as its price moved from ₹705 to ₹2711.

Profit – 2006 Points

October 2019

This series turned out to be flat.

From 30002 to 30066 move was not good enough for anything except causing a loss.

CALL 30000 Buy Price ₹955 Sell Price ₹66

Loss – 889 Points

The 12 month journey from November 2018 to October 2019 was now complete.

This year had elections and its effect on the market, a new finance minister coming to grips with the situation and facing criticism from almost every quarter and the normal overhang of the world markets.

With all that, BANKNIFTY managed to go up from 24817 to 30066 in these 12 months.

ATM Call buying profit for this period was 2654 points with 4 gaining and 8 losing months.

We see that the number of gaining or losing trades does not matter. It is the quantum of gain which is the key to profit.

ITM Calls too did well.

Summary of 12 months:

November 2018- October 2019

Series	BANK-NIFTY at start	BANK-NIFTY at close	ATM Call strike price	Buy Price	Sell Price	Profit/ Loss
November	24817	26939	24800	822	2144	1322
December	26939	26878	26900	453	0	(453)
January	26878	27245	26900	550	380	(170)
February	27245	26789	27200	475	0	(475)
March	26789	30420	26800	631	3600	2969
April	30420	29561	30400	690	0	(690)
May	29561	31537	29600	1025	1914	889
June	31537	31269	31500	635	0	(635)
July	31269	29043	31300	563	0	(563)
August	29043	27309	29000	657	0	(657)
September	27309	30002	27300	705	2711	2006
October	30002	30066	30000	955	66	(889)
Total						2654

ITM Call Option Buying

Series	BANK-NIFTY at start	BANK-NIFTY at close	ITM Call strike price	Buy Price	Sell Price	Profit/ Loss
November	24817	26939	23500	1668	3410	1742
December	26939	26878	25500	1522	1371	(151)
January	26878	27245	25500	1615	1764	149
February	27245	26789	26000	1425	769	(656)
March	26789	30420	25500	1575	4900	3325
April	30420	29561	29000	1671	557	(1014)
May	29561	31537	28000	2020	3526	1506
June	31537	31269	30000	1731	1230	(501)
July	31269	29043	30000	1477	0	(1477)
August	29043	27309	27500	1820	0	(1820)
September	27309	30002	26000	1626	4003	2377
October	30002	30066	28500	1944	1568	(376)
Total						3104

ITM Call options had 5 months of profit for a gain of 3104 points.

The story has now covered 7 years of BANKNIFTY moves and CALL option buying results.

Next year is the one which is still fresh in everyone's memory.

The year that saw the big crash.

The Covid -19 pandemic and its impact on the world markets had sent the markets all over the world into a spin.

The crash of March 2020 will forever be a lesson for the market participants.

We continue with the story and find out how BANKNIFTY CALL buying worked out in those difficult times.

❑

CHAPTER 10

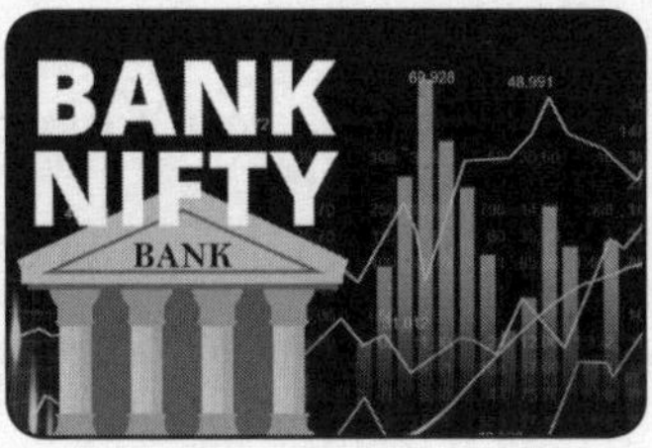

The World Reels under Covid-19 Wave

The announcements made by the Finance Minister were seemingly having some impact on the market.

After a subdued October 2019, BANKNIFTY again came into its own in November series.

November 2019

November 2019 was a good time to be in the market and a good time to buy BANKNIFTY Call option.

BANKNIFTY CALL 30000 went up from ₹760 to ₹2125 as the index soared from 30066 to 32122.

Profit – 1365 Points.

December 2019

A strong month is normally followed by a flat month. This time BAANKNIFTY went down from 32122 to 31997 with the most common result in option buying – a losing trade.

CALL 32000 lost the entire premium amount of ₹682.

Loss – 682 Points.

January 2020

The new year was not a good beginning for BANKNIFTY. It slumped further to 30647.

BANKNIFTY lost 1350 points in this series while CALL 32000 priced at ₹680 became worthless.

Loss – 680 Points.

February 2020

As this series began, there was news about a mysterious virus in Wuhan province in China. People were dying and the entire city was supposedly in a lock down.

Slowly the virus made inroads into Europe and then into USA.

There was unspoken fear as not much was known about the virus at this early stage.

Market is usually ahead of the news. In February 2020 series, BANKNIFTY was flattish while going down to 30187.

Not much of a fall but enough to cause full premium loss of ₹805 in Call 30600.

March 2020

This was the month when everyone took note of the pandemic which by this time had spread all over the world.

There were daily reports of thousands of deaths in Europe, USA, China and India.

Lock downs were ordered everywhere. Flights and other modes of travel were brought to a standstill. The world had come to a stop.

No cause, no cure for the virus was a menacing truth.

As the governments all over the world struggled with managing the effects of pandemic, stock markets crashed.

In March 2020 series, we saw BANKNIFTY moving down from 30187 to 19613.

On March 24, 2020, BANKNIFTY had touched the low of 16116.25.

Even after the recovery from the low, the fall in this series was 35.02%.

Such falls take away many years of investment profits.

For the Call buyer, it can take away only the premium paid.

CALL 30200 which was priced at ₹660 at the beginning of series ended up worthless.

Loss – 660 Points.

April 2020

Market showed very good resilience and with the Covid-19 pandemic playing havoc, there was a decent recovery in April series.

BANKNIFTY moved up from 19613 to 21534.

In view of the huge volatility seen in March, option premiums had hit the roof.

CALL 19600 was atrociously priced at ₹1800.

It closed at 1933 for a small gain of ₹133.

Profit – 133 Points.

May 2020

The good work of April series came unstuck in May.

BANKNIFTY gave up all the gains of previous month to go back to 19169. This level was lower than the March 2020 series closing level.

CALL 21500 lost the premium amount of ₹907.

Loss – 907 Points.

June 2020

There was not much change on the pandemic front. Some of the travel restrictions were lifted. Lock down was not forced at this stage but people were not venturing out due to fear.

Market ignored the negatives and BANKNIFTY once again made an upward push to close at 21506.

From 19169 to 21506 was a move almost the reverse of previous month.

CALL 19200 moved up from ₹790 to ₹2288.

Profit – 1498 points.

We see that with almost identical moves in either direction, the loss in May was 907 points whereas profit in June was 1498 points.

This is the edge what makes option buying profitable.

But to get the benefit from that edge, one has to stay the course. Big profit does not come without big patience.

July 2020

A small move in this series took BANKNIFTY from 21506 to 21646.

Small moves do not make money.

CALL 21500 went from ₹1152 to ₹147.

Loss – 1105 points

August 2020

BANKNIFTY retrieved some more of the lost ground in August series as it moved from 21646 to 23600.

A good move.

CALL 21600 moved up from ₹790 to ₹2288.

Profit – 1498 Points

September 2020

There was a big fall in September.

BANKNIFTY went down from 23600 to 20456.

Another incident of a CALL option becoming worthless.

CALL 23600 Buy Price ₹755 Sell Price 0

Loss – 755 Points.

October 2020

The pandemic was still there.

If the fall in September can be attributed to the pandemic, there was no reason for the market to rally. But the market moves in a strange way.

BANKNIFTY made a big up move in October series.

It moved from 20456 to 24092.

This 3636-points rally saw CALL 20500 go up from ₹933 to ₹3600.

This was real big deal.

Profit – 2667 points.

Summary of 12 Months

A crash followed by some recovery. Out of 12 months, 5 were profitable. The big fall of March 2020 caused a loss of 660 points only. We can see that over this period, BANKNIFTY had actually moved lower from 30066 to 24092, losing 5974 points.

Still, ATM CALL option buying made a profit of 1270 points.

ITM Call option buying resulted in a profit of 929 points with 5 successful months.

November 2019- October 2020

Series	BANK-NIFTY at start	BANK-NIFTY at close	ATM Call strike price	Buy Price	Sell Price	Profit/ Loss
November	30066	32122	30000	760	2125	1365
December	32122	31997	32000	682	0	(682)
January	31997	30647	32000	680	0	(680)
February	30647	30187	30600	805	0	(805)

March	30187	19613	30200	660	0	(660)
April	19613	21534	19600	1800	1933	133
May	21534	19169	21500	907	0	(907)
June	19169	21506	19200	790	2288	1498
July	21506	21646	21500	1152	147	(1005)
August	21646	23600	21600	900	2001	1101
September	23600	20456	23600	755	0	(755)
October	20456	24092	20500	933	3600	2667
Total						1270

ITM Call Option Buying

Series	BANK-NIFTY at start	BANK-NIFTY at close	ITM Call strike price	Buy Price	Sell Price	Profit/ Loss
November	30066	32122	28500	1765	3628	1853
December	32122	31997	30500	1793	1504	(289)
January	31997	30647	30500	1827	147	(1680)
February	30647	30187	29000	1888	1192	(696)
March	30187	19613	28500	1860	0	(1860)

April	19613	21534	18500	2600	3023	423
May	21534	19169	20500	1452	0	(1452)
June	19169	21506	18000	1511	3507	1996
July	21506	21646	20500	1700	1150	(550)
August	21646	23600	20500	1533	3096	1563
September	23600	20456	22500	1438	0	(1438)
October	20456	24092	19500	1525	4584	3059
Total						929

These results show that CALL buying could make money even when the index was down in a big way over the one year period.

It is the randomness of the moves which gives a profit or loss.

In the period Nov 2014-Oct 2015, the randomness worked against Call buying which resulted in a big loss.

This year, trades benefited from same random moves.

We should not formulate a theory based on these results even though temptation is huge.

In the same period, any trader buying PUT options also would have made a handsome profit.

This is something which rarely happens. CALL and PUT buyers both making money over the same time frame of 12 months.

The journey of a PUT buyer will be covered in another chapter.

The Call buying story now moves into ninth year.

❑

CHAPTER 11

Dream Comes True

BANKNIFTY was down 5974 points over last 12 months yet CALL buying could get a profit.

Before we discuss the course of events for next 12 months, we look at the summary of results of previous 8 years.

Year November-October	ATM Call Option Points	ATM Call Profit Months	ITM Call Option Points	ITM Call Profit Months
2012-13	1141	5	311	7
2013-14	2368	6	3733	8

2014-15	(2051)	3	(1359)	4
2015-16	694	5	2017	7
2016-17	3563	7	4733	8
2017-18	1341	5	856	6
2018-19	2654	4	3104	5
2019-20	1270	5	929	5
Total	10980	40	14324	50

In 8 years, BANKNIFTY after all the ups and downs had moved from 11614 to 24092.

Total index gain = 12478 Points.

The results of CALL buying are trying to give us a very strong message. It is for us to decipher the truth and act on the facts in future.

ATM Call buying could capture 10980 of those 12478 points.

ITM Call buying did much better as it notched up 14324 points, far more than what the index gained.

We have two more years to go.

There could be losses to spoil the impact of these numbers. Or things could get better.

November 2020

If we thought that the October series move from 20456 to 24092 was a good move, November series had something much better in store. BANKNIFTY was on steroids in this series as it went from strength to strength and the closing happened at 29549.

This series had a gain of 5457 points.

These types of moves are an option buyer's dream.

CALL 24100 price moved from ₹1039 to ₹5565.

Profit – 4526 points.

To get this profit, one has to stay with the trade till end, not book a part profit and exit.

December 2020

BANKNIFTY was in a hurry to get back to the levels seen before the mayhem caused by Covid-19.

In December series, index moved from 29549 to 31264.

CALL 29500 Buy Price ₹1198 Sell Price 1765

Profit – 567 Points

January 2021

In December 2019, BANKNIFTY had closed at 31997.

In December 2020, BANKNIFTY closed at 31264.

In one year, it went deep into the pits in March 2020 and came out by December 2020.

Any investor with BANKNIFTY ETF would not have any money in these 12 months but the CALL buying would have earned very good profits.

We continue with the action in January 2021 series.

The first month of the new year saw BANKNIFTY backtracking to 30358.

CALL 31300 Buy Price ₹980 Sell Price ₹0

Loss – 980 Points

February 2021

BANKNIFTY outdid its November series performance in February.

This time the move was from 30358 to 36549. The gain was 6191 points.

CALL 30300 Buy Price – ₹1125 Sell Price – ₹5975

Profit – 4850 Points

One could do with few more months of such gains.

March 2021

Fortune turns like a wheel.

One moment, You are up next moment, you are down in the dirt.

BANKNIFTY fell from 36549 to 33006.

CALL 36500 with an initial price of ₹1236 became worthless.

Loss – 1236 Points.

April 2021

April series was a slow grind compared to the swift moves over previous two months.

BANKNIFTY found its way to 33714 from 33006.

CALL 33000 lost some money as its price went down from ₹1396 to ₹714.

Loss – 682 Points.

May 2021

May series saw another up move which did not give much benefit for buying a CALL option.

BANKNIFTY moved higher from 33714 to 35095 and CALL 33700 had its price going from ₹1207 to ₹1395.

Profit – 188 Points.

June 2021

There was a small down move in BANKNIFTY in June series as it went down from 35095 to 34827.

Small move or big move, on the downside both are same for the CALL buyer.

CALL 35100 priced at ₹1269 became worthless.

Loss – 1269 Points.

July 2021

Another month similar to previous month with BANKNIFTY going down from 34827 to 34691.

Another loss as CALL 34700 with a price of ₹785 became worthless.

Loss – 785 Points.

August 2021

Some recovery in BANKNIFTY saw it move up to 35617.

CALL 34700 price went up from ₹785 to ₹917.

Profit – 132 Points

September 2021

After few months of small moves, some improvement was seen in September series as BANKNIFTY moved up from 35617 to 37425.

CALL 35600 Buy Price ₹765 Sell Price ₹1874

Profit – 1109 Points

October 2021

There was another upsurge in October as BANKNIFTY scaled new heights and closed at 39508.

CALL 37400 Buy Price ₹1050 Sell Price ₹2109

Profit – 1059 Points

Summary of 12 Months

In the period November 2020- October 2021, BANKNIFTY moved up from 24092 to 39508.

The 15416 points (63.98%) gain in 12 months is just fantastic. We are not likely to see such gains again in a hurry.

This chapter was titled based on these numbers.

How much was the gain from buying CALL options?

And what was the result of buying ITM Call options?

The numbers are tabulated here:

November 2020 - December 2021

Series	BANK-NIFTY at start	BANK-NIFTY at close	ATM Call strike price	Buy Price	Sell Price	Profit/Loss
November	24092	29549	24100	1039	5565	4526
December	29549	31264	29500	1198	1765	567
January	31264	30358	31300	980	0	(980)
February	30358	36549	30300	1125	5975	4850
March	36549	33006	36500	1236	0	(1236)
April	33006	33714	33000	1396	714	(682)
May	33714	35095	33700	1207	1395	188
June	35095	34827	35100	1269	0	(1269)
July	34827	34691	34800	986	0	(986)
August	34691	35617	34700	785	917	132
September	35617	37425	35600	765	1874	1109
October	37425	39508	37400	1050	2109	1059
Total						7278

ATM Call option buying profit for the 12 months was 7278 points.

Trades were profitable in 7 out of 12 months.

There were two big payoffs in November 2020 and February 2021.

The overall profit is less than the profit of these two months.

This again puts emphasis on the fact that taking the big profits (when the market gives) is a must.

Option sellers can make a living taking small profits (I have my doubts but most people believe this to be true) but option buyers will face losses if they miss out on big profits.

Results of ITM Call buying

The profit was much better at 10869 points.

It captured 70.50% of the BANKNIFTY move over this 12 months period.

There were 7 months of profit, same as for ATM Call options.

It goes without saying that profits of 4886 points in November 2020 and 5651 points in February 2021 were the key numbers.

ITM Call Option Buying

Series	BANK-NIFTY at Start	BANK-NIFTY at Close	ITM Call Strike Price	Buy Price	Sell Price	Profit/ Loss
November	24092	29549	23000	1679	6555	4886
December	29549	31264	28000	2149	3268	1119
January	31264	30358	30000	1744	361	(1383)
February	30358	36549	29000	1904	7555	5651
March	36549	33006	35000	2160	0	(2160)
April	33006	33714	31500	2361	2218	(143)
May	33714	35095	32000	2300	3099	799
June	35095	34827	33500	2346	1326	(1020)
July	34827	34691	33000	2285	1697	(588)
August	34691	35617	33000	2060	2615	555
September	35617	37425	34000	1928	3451	1523
October	37425	39508	35500	2350	3980	1630
Total						10869

I wish I could close the story here on a high note.

Nothing beats the euphoria of a big score in option buying.

This chapter was about the dream coming true for option buyers.

There is a problem with dreams.

They come to an end when you wake up.

And one cannot remain in a dreamy state forever.

As I write, I remember the title of a novel by Harold Robbins which I read four decades ago – **DREAMS DIE FIRST.**

We continue the story into its tenth year and see whether the dream run continued or came to a halt.

❑

CHAPTER 12

Waking Up To Reality

This is the most recent part of the story.

Readers would be more familiar with the moves made by the index in these 12 months.

November 2021

After closing at 39508 in October series, November was a setback for BANKNIFTY.

It fell to 37364.

CALL 39500 priced at ₹1062 ended up worthless.

Loss – 1062 Points

December 2021

Further fall was waiting for us in December series and BANKNIFTY tumbled from 37364 to 35063.

It had taken two months to move from 35617 to 39508.

In another two months, index was back to 35063.

This is normal. Market can do only two things go up or down. We stay calm with whatever is happening.

Our maximum loss is known at the time of entering the trade.

This month ended up with that maximum loss as CALL 37400 turned worthless from its buy price of ₹885.

Loss – 885 Points.

January 2022

BANKNIFTY welcomed the new year with an up move as it moved from 35063 to 37962.

CALL 35000 priced at ₹1009 moved up to ₹2985. Profit – 1976 Points.

February 2022

Premiums were high for February series because of Union Budget presentation. The price of ₹1318 for CALL

38000 was ultimately worth nothing as BANKNIFTY moved lower to 35228.

Loss – 1318 Points.

March 2022

From October 2021 expiry to February 2022 expiry, BANKNIFTY had come down 4280 points.

Those looking for an up move got it in March series.

The move was from 35228 to 36373, not good enough to be profitable.

Premium for CALL 35200 went down from 1400 to 1175.

Loss – 225 Points.

April 2022

Sad story of BANKNIFTY moving lower or staying flat and CALL buying ending up with a loss continued in April series.

BANKNIFTY moved from 36373 to 36422 while CALL 36400 ended up at ₹21 from its initial price of ₹1078.

Loss – 1057 Points.

May 2022

May was not different.

Sell in May and go away worked out for sellers this time. Call buyers had to face a loss as BANKNIFTY went down to 35094 level.

CALL 36400 Buy Price – ₹935 Sell Price – ₹0

Loss – 935 Points

June 2022

The worst was not over.

Another decline was in waiting for June 2022 series.

BANKNIFTY went down to 33425 from the previous series closing of 35094.

CALL 35000 lost the entire premium of ₹1180 as it became worthless.

Loss – 1180 Points.

July 2022

What was the name of the book – DREAMS DIE FIRST.

The last five months could be called DREAMS DIE FAST.

If someone had not seen the wonderful profits of few months ago, one would not talk of option buying being profitable with the kind of results seen now.

Option buyers need the patience of a monk.

July series rewarded the patience as BANKNIFTY woke up from its slumber and raced to 37378.

CALL 33400 moved to ₹3975 from its buy price of ₹870.

Profit – 3105 Points.

August 2022

The up move continued in August as BANKNIFTY traversed the journey from 37378 to 38950.

CALL 37400 price went up from ₹752 to ₹1549.

Profit – 797 Points

September 2022

BANKNIFTY took a break in September and moved lower to 37647.

CALL 39000 became worthless and premium of ₹865 was lost.

Loss – 865 Points.

October 2022

BANKNIFTY had taken a breather in September. It came out firing on all cylinders in October series and breached 41000 level to close at 41299. It was a 3652 point move.

Good for the Call buyers.

CALL – 37600 Buy Price – ₹1196 Sell Price – ₹3723.

Profit – 2527 Points.

The dream that looked like ending at the beginning of July series continued its run.

The numbers for the 12-months period are tabulated here:

November 2021- December 2022

Series	BANK-NIFTY at start	BAN-K-NIFTY at close	ATM Call strike price	Buy Price	Sell Price	Profit/ Loss
November	39508	37364	39500	1062	0	(1062)
December	37364	35063	37400	885	0	(885)
January	35063	37962	35000	1009	2985	1976
February	37962	35228	38000	1318	0	(1318)
March	35228	36373	35200	1400	1175	(225)

April	36373	36422	36400	1078	21	(1057)
May	36422	35094	36400	935	0	(935)
June	35094	33425	35000	1180	0	(1180)
July	33425	37378	33400	870	3975	3105
August	37378	38950	37400	752	1549	797
September	38950	37647	39000	865	0	(865)
October	37647	41299	37600	1196	3723	2527
Total						878

Not a great result compared to previous 12 months period but still a profit.

There was a time when it looked like a certain loss but the up move in BANKNIFTY in July and October 2022 took care of that fear.

There were only 4 months of profit out of 12.

Every year will not give similar results.

One year we may have a feast, another year we may starve.

It is the surplus from the feasting that will carry us through the starvation period.

Results for ITM Call Buying

Surprisingly ITM Call option buying lost money in these 12 months. And the loss was big.

I had mentioned about anomalies earlier in the book. The performance in these months was one more such occasion.

ITM Call Option Buying

Series	BANK-NIFTY at Start	BANK-NIFTY at Close	ITM Call Strike Price	Buy Price	Sell Price	Profit/ Loss
November	39508	37364	37500	2500	0	(2500)
December	37364	35063	35500	2235	0	(2235)
January	35063	37962	33500	2053	4460	2407
February	37962	35228	36000	2672	0	(2672)
March	35228	36373	33500	2431	2827	446
April	36373	36422	34500	2400	1926	(474)
May	36422	35094	34500	2259	597	(1662)
June	35094	33425	33500	2205	0	(2205)
July	33425	37378	32000	1750	5380	3630
August	37378	38950	35500	2109	3451	1342
September	38950	37647	37000	2212	622	(1590)

October	37647	41299	36000	2266	5310	3034
Total						(2479)

There was profit in 5 out of 12 months but not enough to cover the loss in other 7 months.

This concludes the ten year journey of CALL option buying in BANKNIFTY index from November 2012 to October 2022.

It is now time to come to some conclusions based on the numbers seen over these ten years. We shall do that in the next chapter.

❑

CHAPTER 13

Did We Find the Key to Profit?

The quest for finding a winning strategy is eternal. We are so taken up with that goal, that we fail to appreciate the opportunities that are just there to explore.

The simple act of buying a BANKNIFTY Call option, whether it is an ATM option or deep ITM option, gave wonderful results over the ten years period.

I am certain that if we go back few more years, the results would be similar.

The best thing would be to trust these results and take advantage of the index moving higher in the years to come.

Past is a mirror in which we can see the future.

In 10 years, BANKNIFTY had moved from 11614 to 41299.

It gained 29685 points i.e., 255.59%

We now look at the CALL option buying performance.

Year November-October	ATM Call Option Points	ATM Call Profit Months	ITM Call Option Points	ITM Call Profit Months
2012-13	1141	5	311	7
2013-14	2368	6	3733	8
2014-15	(2051)	3	(1359)	4
2015-16	694	5	2017	7
2016-17	3563	7	4733	8
2017-18	1341	5	856	6
2018-19	2654	4	3104	5
2019-20	1270	5	929	5
2020-21	7278	7	10869	7
2021-22	878	4	(2479)	5
Total	19136	51	22714	62

ATM Call option buying was profitable in 51 months out of 120.

That is a success rate of 42.5%.

This is good success for option buyer. Only caveat being that we have to grab as many big profits as the market is willing to give. Patience is the key in such situations.

ITM Call buying had better success at 62 months out of 120 being profitable. That is 51.66% which is again good.

ATM CALL buying captured 19136 points out of total BANKNIFTY gain of 29685 points while ITM Call buying got 22714 points.

In Chapter -3, we had mentioned that we need a trading capital of about 15 times the option premium and had worked out the starting capital as ₹125000 ten years ago.

As the entire discussion has been based on BANKNIFTY points, we take the capital as 5000 points.

Capital – 5000 Points

Profit from ATM Call options – 19136 points

Profit = 382.72%

Capital requirement would be similar for ITM call option buying.

We take it as 6 months premium at the beginning.

Considering that the first premium was 738 points in November 2012 series, this requirement comes to 6 x 738 = 4428 points.

We round it off to 5000 points for some additional cushion.

Capital – 5000 Points

Profit from ITM Call options – 22714 points

Profit = 454.28%

As most of the traders would not be very comfortable with ITM Call options due to bigger cash outflow every month while buying the option, we shall make comparison with the ATM Call results only.

Call option buying gave far better results than BANKNIFTY return of **255.59%.**

If we compare with some prominent banking stocks, the result still looks very good.

HDFCBANK – 356%, ICICIBANK –372%, AXISBANK – 269%, SBIN – 163%, CANBK -227% have all given returns lower than Call option buying.

Only KOTAKBANK with 496% gain in 10 years did better.

I know that readers will mention about dividend income for stocks in this period and that would be a valid point.

But if you were invested in YESBANK, UNIONBANK, PNB or BNKBARODA, the loss would have been 81%, 73%, 74% and 2% respectively.

And more investors end up in losing stocks than in the multi baggers.

This is why it is appropriate to compare with the index which is a summation of both good and bad stocks.

And CALL buying performed much better than BANKNIFTY.

Have we actually found the key to profit?

The profit was there all the time.

The bias against option buying is so strong that we do not give it a proper look.

Everyone talks about options expiring worthless.

Nobody tries to find out the outcome when they give a profit.

We have now seen that the profit can be very good.

Option sellers take small profits. If option buyers fall in the trap of small profits, they are playing a game with different set of rules and will surely end up making losses.

Different strokes for different folks.

Many readers will have the question – What if the gains in 2021-22 had not happened?

Answer – Had BANKNIFTY not gained in 2021-22, probably it would have gained at some other time.

And all others, investors in ETF, mutual funds, banking stocks, would not have made money if the gain in 2021-22 not happened.

I hope that with these results in hand and hammered repeatedly at the risk of being boring, traders will now look at option buying differently and positively.

❑

CHAPTER 14

Putting it Across – Buying PUT Options

We began with the shared information that buying both CALL and PUT options was profitable in year 2019 and 2020.

There are Black Swan funds which make profit after a gap of few years whenever some big crash happens.

But can a trader survive by buying ATM PUT options every month?

Or by buying a combination of CALL and PUT options?

Let us verify the numbers and make it a fact-based discussion.

One thing is sure – PUT trade can not make money when the CALL trade does.

But both trades can lose money in the same month.

ATM Call options made a profit in 51 out of 120 months.

We shall not go for a month by month detailing in case of ATM PUT options but look at one year time period at a glance.

November 2012-October 2013:

Series	BANK-NIFTY at Start	BANK-NIFTY at Close	ATM PUT Strike Price	Buy Price	Sell Price	Profit/ Loss
November	11614	11992	11600	208	0	(208)
December	11992	12459	12000	190	0	(190)
January	12459	12708	12500	210	0	(210)
February	12708	11487	12700	186	1230	1044

March	11487	11361	11500	149	129	(20)
April	11361	12726	11400	200	0	(200)
May	12726	12805	12700	350	0	(350)
June	12805	11235	12800	300	1555	1255
July	11235	10614	11200	241	575	334
August	10614	8904	10600	300	1700	1400
September	8904	10098	8900	379	0	(379)
October	10098	11473	10100	415	0	(415)
Total						2061

The first one year of ATM PUT buying had 4 profit making months. The profit was good enough to offset the loss of other 8 months.

Net profit in 12 months – 2061 Points.

Second year was not so good.

November 2013- October 2014:

Series	BANK-NIFTY at Start	BANK-NIFTY at Close	ATM PUT Strike Price	Buy Price	Sell Price	Profit/ Loss
November	11473	10906	11500	310	592	282
December	10906	11385	10900	299	0	(299)

January	11385	10153	11400	275	1240	965
February	10153	10730	10200	270	0	(270)
March	10730	12804	10700	213	0	(213)
April	12804	13122	12800	425	0	(425)
May	13122	15030	13100	655	0	(655)
June	15030	15050	15000	403	0	(403)
July	15050	15267	15000	392	0	(392)
August	15267	15740	15300	281	0	(281)
September	15740	15299	15700	287	390	103
October	15299	16760	15300	410	0	(410)
Total						(1998)

With 3 profits and 9 losses, this year ended up with a loss of 1998 points.

After two years of buying ATM PUT options there was a profit of just 63 points.

Not a great way to go.

November 2014- October 2015

ATM Call buying had made a loss in this 12-months period.

Apparently, ATM PUT buying should have made some profit.

It was not like that.

With 3 profits and 9 losses, there was a loss of 817 points.

This was a period when it did not matter whether you bought CALLS or PUTS. Money was lost doing both.

When such a thing happens, nobody posts a video about it on YouTube.

Series	**BANK-NIFTY at Start**	**BANK-NIFTY at Close**	**ATM PUT Strike Price**	**Buy Price**	**Sell Price**	**Profit/ Loss**
November	16760	18022	16800	325	0	(325)
December	18022	18535	18000	318	0	(318)
January	18535	20528	18500	319	0	(319)
February	20528	18538	20500	504	1974	1470
March	18538	17831	18500	480	690	210
April	17831	18338	17800	280	0	(280)
May	18338	18449	18300	320	0	(320)
June	18449	18492	18400	442	0	(442)

July	18492	18440	18500	453	60	(393)
August	18440	17214	18400	365	1165	800
September	17214	17196	17200	414	3	(411)
October	17196	17212	17200	489	0	(489)
Total						(817)

With 3 years gone, ATM PUT option buying had gone into a loss, the total loss being 754 points.

The loss was not too big and one big down move could wipe it out completely.

Options buyers are forever hopeful. They keep trudging along.

Let us see whether their hopes of a profit were realized in the fourth year.

November 2015 – October 2016

There were 2 small losses in the beginning followed by 2 good profits. After that, there were 8 consecutive losses.

Only 2 profitable months out of 12 could not prevent a loss for the year which worked out to 528 points.

PUT buying was not working out as is evident from these numbers.

Series	BANK-NIFTY at Start	BANK-NIFTY at Close	ATM PUT Strike Price	Buy Price	Sell Price	Profit/ Loss
November	17212	17036	17200	375	165	(210)
December	17036	16922	17000	343	81	(262)
January	16922	15381	16900	291	1550	1259
February	15381	13555	15400	366	1832	1466
March	13555	16141	13600	425	0	(425)
April	16141	16716	16100	350	0	(350)
May	16716	17359	16700	365	0	(365)
June	17359	17935	17400	462	0	(462)
July	17935	19076	17900	313	0	(313)
August	19076	19304	19000	322	0	(322)
September	19304	19183	19300	314	120	(194)
October	19183	19514	19200	350	0	(350)
Total						(528)

In 4 years of ATM PUT buying, the loss had mounted to 1282 points.

November 2016 – October 2017

We had seen in the ATM CALL buying details that these 12 months had given a very good profit. For most part of the year, BANKNIFTY had moved higher. It was not a surprise to find out that ATM PUT buying once again failed to make a profit.

There were only 2 months which saw a profit while other 10 months contributed to the loss.

Total loss for the Year 5 was 1943 points.

Traders always face this dilemma of making a decision while facing adversity. There maybe people who wait five years to make a profit but everyone is not that people.

And with accumulated loss of 3225 points over five years, one would have to be a Braveheart to continue.

Before we find out what happened by continuing with the trades, here is the poor performance of Year 5.

November 2016 – October 2017

Series	BANK NIFTY at Start	BANK NIFTY at Close	ATM PUT Strike Price	Buy Price	Sell Price	Profit/ Loss
November	19514	18256	19500	318	1250	932
December	18256	18033	18300	403	245	(158)

January	18033	19473	18000	300	0	(300)
February	19473	20876	19500	395	0	(395)
March	20876	21620	20900	424	0	(424)
April	21620	22326	21600	379	0	(379)
May	22326	23190	22300	332	0	(332)
June	23190	23227	23200	450	0	(450)
July	23227	24922	23200	324	0	(324)
August	24922	24318	25000	389	664	275
September	24318	24008	24300	329	292	(37)
October	24008	25022	24000	351	0	(351)
Total						(1943)

November 2017- October 2018:

Option buying does not result into a single big loss. The losses accumulate slowly. In between there are some profits which give the sense that eventually a profit can be made.

In the next 12 months, tide turned for PUT buyers.

Index did not move much but there were enough down moves which resulted in decent profits.

There was profit in 4 months with 1860 points and 2719 points coming in February and September series respectively.

These good numbers ensure that there was a profit of 1762 points at the end of 12 months.

This was another instance of both ATM Call options and ATM PUT options making profit in the same 12 months period.

ATM PUT buying was still making losses after 6 years, net loss being 1463 points.

November 2017- October 2018

Series	BANK-NIFTY at Start	BANK-NIFTY at Close	ATM PUT Strike Price	Buy Price	Sell Price	Profit/ Loss
November	25022	25332	25000	393	0	(393)
December	25332	25490	25300	325	0	(325)
January	25490	27445	25500	340	0	(340)
February	27445	24955	27400	550	2410	1860
March	24955	24263	25000	500	710	210
April	24263	25010	24300	440	0	(440)
May	25010	26956	25000	421	0	(421)
June	26956	26324	27000	565	669	104

July	26324	27406	26300	456	0	(456)
August	27406	28103	27400	499	0	(499)
September	28103	25042	28100	347	3066	2719
October	25042	24817	25000	441	184	(257)
Total						1762

November 2018- October 2019

Previous 12 months had shown a profit which brought down the overall loss from ATM PUT option buying.

It was back to earlier trend of PUT options causing a loss at the end of this 12 months period.

There were 3 months of profits which could not wipe out the loss incurred over other 9 months.

The loss for the year was 1135 points.

It seems our market does not care for the Black Swans.

Seven years of ATM PUT option buying in BANKNIFTY and still a loss to show for all our efforts.

The loss at the end of seven years was 2598 points.

November 2018- October 2019

Series	BANK-NIFTY at Start	BANK-NIFTY at Close	ATM PUT Strike Price	Buy Price	Sell Price	Profit/ Loss
November	24817	26939	24800	614	0	(614)
December	26939	26878	26900	481	0	(481)
January	26878	27245	26900	430	0	(430)
February	27245	26789	27200	422	400	(22)
March	26789	30420	26800	440	0	(440)
April	30420	29561	30400	560	812	252
May	29561	31537	29600	895	0	(895)
June	31537	31269	31500	500	192	(308)
July	31269	29043	31300	480	2220	1736
August	29043	27309	29000	396	1681	1285
September	27309	30002	27300	525	0	(525)
October	30002	30066	30000	693	0	(693)
Total						(1135)

November 2019- October 2020

Finally the BLACK SWAN was sighted.

It happened in March 2020.

BANKNIFTY crashed from 30187 to 19613.

And PUT 30200 moved from ₹587 to ₹10586.

Profit – 9999 points.

Market had rewarded the patience of the persistent PUT buyers and wiped out all the loss accumulated over previous seven years.

But were there any actual traders booking this kind of profit?

I seriously doubt it. But it was possible with the simple act of buying an option and then DOING NOTHING about it.

There was profit in 4 out of 12 months.

This was the year when people started posting about BANKNIFTY STRADDLE buying being very profitable.

November 2019 – October 2020

Series	BANK-NIFTY at Start	BANK-NIFTY at Close	ATM PUT Strike Price	Buy Price	Sell Price	Profit/ Loss
November	30066	32122	30000	701	0	(701)
December	32122	31997	32000	528	0	(528)

January	31997	30647	32000	509	1356	847
February	30647	30187	30600	680	413	(267)
March	30187	19613	30200	587	10586	9999
April	19613	21534	19600	2000	0	(2000)
May	21534	19169	21500	1099	2330	1231
June	19169	21506	19200	1010	0	(1010)
July	21506	21646	21500	1210	0	(1210)
August	21646	23600	21600	890	0	(890)
September	23600	20456	23600	752	3143	2391
October	20456	24092	20500	890	0	(890)
Total						6972

With 6972 points added in this year, profit at the end of 8 years comes to 4374 points.

Finally, ATM PUT option buying became profitable after 96 months. It was profitable after first 12 months also.

The timing of the profit is dependent on the market moves.

November 2020-October 2021

This was the period when markets had staged a full recovery and NIFTY had started making new record highs. BANKNIFTY was bit of a laggard but still it was a big gainer over this period.

The extent of loss through ATM PUT options was quite big and almost took away the entire profit of previous 12 months.

With only 1 profitable month out of 12, this year ended up with a loss of 6456 points.

Not a great advertisement for ATM PUT buying.

November 2020- October 2021

Series	BANK-NIFTY at Start	BANK-NIFTY at Close	ATM PUT Strike Price	Buy Price	Sell Price	Profit/ Loss
November	24092	29549	24100	1035	0	(1035)
December	29549	31264	29500	1047	0	(1047)
January	31264	30358	31300	960	841	(119)
February	30358	36549	30300	1000	0	(1000)
March	36549	33006	36500	1011	3498	2487
April	33006	33714	33000	1110	0	(1110)
May	33714	35095	33700	1190	0	(1190)
June	35095	34827	35100	983	273	(710)
July	34827	34691	34800	750	107	(643)

August	34691	35617	34700	596	0	(596)
September	35617	37425	35600	661	0	(661)
October	37425	39508	37400	832	0	(832)
Total						(6456)

November 2021- December 2022

PUT option buying was showing a profit at the end of 8 years. Year 9 changed the picture.

It was back to losses again.

The loss amount being 2082 points.

We were now into year number 10.

In these 12 months, there were 6 profits and 6 losses.

With these numbers, there was a profit of 552 points for the year.

Not a very big number but any profit is welcome.

This year was another case of profit being possible from ATM CALL option buying as well as ATM PUT option buying.

November 2021- December 2022

Series	BANK-NIFTY at Start	BANK-NIFTY at Close	ATM PUT Strike Price	Buy Price	Sell Price	Profit/ Loss
November	39508	37364	39500	871	2137	1266
December	37364	35063	37400	712	2340	1628
January	35063	37962	35000	715	0	(715)
February	37962	35228	38000	1019	2778	1759
March	35228	36373	35200	1499	0	(1499)
April	36373	36422	36400	946	0	(946)
May	36422	35094	36400	838	1305	467
June	35094	33425	35000	918	1575	657
July	33425	37378	33400	913	0	(913)
August	37378	38950	37400	725	0	(725)
September	38950	37647	39000	895	1352	457
October	37647	41299	37600	884	0	(884)
Total						552

The loss after 10 years through ATM PUT buying comes to 1530 points.

What do we conclude from these numbers?

There may be a big profit from PUT options in case of a huge down move in a particular time period. That profit can wipe out the losses sustained over 5-6 years.

But buying PUT options regularly goes against the fact – Markets move higher over a long period of time.

Making profits by trading with a contrarian view is possible but one has to go with long periods of losses.

Most of the traders do not have the patience to go through these long losing spells.

And the numbers do not make a case for PUT buying.

❑

CHAPTER 15

Do Straddles Really Work?

Ten years of ATM Call option buying resulted in a good profit.

Same ten years of ATM PUT option buying resulted in a small loss.

If we combine the two results, we end up with a net profit.

Easy conclusion – Buying a straddle is profitable over a long period.

For arriving at a proper conclusion, we need to have a look at the numbers.

Year	ATM Call Buy Profit	Number of Profit Months	ATM PUT Buy Profit	Number of Profit Months	Straddle Profit	Number of Profit Months
1	1141	5	2061	4	3202	9
2	2368	6	(1998)	3	370	9
3	(2051)	3	(817)	3	(2868)	6
4	694	5	(528)	2	166	7
5	3563	7	(1943)	2	1620	9
6	1341	5	1762	4	3103	9
7	2654	4	(1135)	3	1519	7
8	1270	5	6972	4	8242	9
9	7278	7	(6456)	1	822	8
10	878	4	552	6	1430	10
Total	19136	51	(1530)	32	17606	83

Buying the straddle was profitable on 83 occasions out of 120. This is a very good success rate of 69.16%.

Traders look at the frequency of the profits not at the real amounts.

Consistent profit gives a false sense of being in a good place. Overall profit is actually less as monthly cash outflow is almost double for buying both CALL and PUT options.

Buying CALL options alone gives much better returns though frequency of profits is on the lower side.

If you are among those who would like to see the profits coming with better frequency, you can opt for buying straddles.

Remember, there are traders out there who make regular profit while SELLING the straddles. They take a small profit and exit the trades. You do the exact opposite. Stay with the trade till the trade sends you out. You get either a profit or a loss.

If we are able to get a profit on about 65-70% occasions as shown in ten years results, it will surely be profitable.

Art of Doing Nothing

As we come to the end of this story, let us sum it up by stating the obvious once again.

Markets move higher over a long period of time – Call buying should be profitable.

Option buying has the potential for UNLIMITED profit – Call buying should be profitable.

Option buying has LIMITED loss – Losses will be less than the potential profits.

Combine these three facts and it makes a solid case for buying any index options.

In India market, it is either NIFTY or BANKNIFTY.

Combine these three facts and the results for ten years listed in this book- that makes a still better case for buying Call options.

In ten years BANKNIFTY has moved up 255%.

It may repeat the move over next 10 years.

Do not miss the next ride to profitability.

DOING NOTHING works.

Let it work for you.

Let BANKNIFTY CALL options add money to your trading account year after year.

Now the standard disclaimer:

Derivatives trading should not be done without knowledge of t\he actual and implied risks. Trading should be done within limits as losses can be huge. Take advice from certified financial *expert before entering the trades. Examples shown here are from the data of previous years and similar performance in future is not assured.*

The author has made the efforts to keep the data as accurate as possible. No responsibility is assumed for any inadvertent errors in the data.

❑